UNDONE

a fakebook

unDONE

a fakebook

Chris McCreary

A Furniture Press Book

FURNITURE PRESS BOOKS
Edited by Christophe Casamassima

First Furniture Press Edition 2010
Copyright © 2010 by Chris McCreary
All Rights Reserved

Except for brief passages quoted in a newspaper, magazine, radio, or television review, no part of this book may be reproduced in any form or by any means, electronic or mechanical, including photocopying and recording, or by any information storage and retrieval system without permission in writing from the publisher.

ACKNOWLEDGMENTS: Some of these poems were previously published in *Columbia Poetry Review* and *Mad Poets Review* and online at *EOAGH*, *Eratio Postmodern Poetry*, *Fanzine*, *Gloom Cupboard*, *Tool: A Magazine*, and *Turntable & Blue Light*. "The Black Book" was also published as an online e-chapbook by Scantily Clad Press.

Cover Art & Layout by Dan Shepelavy
http://shepelavy.com
dan@shepelavy.com

Manufactured in the United States of America

Library of Congress Control Number: 2010922783
ISBN 10: 0-9826299-1-5
ISBN 13: 978-0-9826299-1-8

Furniture Press Books is published for Towson Arts Collective, a not-for-profit corporation under section 501(c)3 United States Internal Revenue Code.

Furniture Press Books
c/o Towson Arts Collective
406 York Road (lower level), Towson, MD 21204
furniture.press.books@gmail.com

Table of Contents
___

Black Star

More Songs about Buildings & Food

The Diamond Sutra

The Great American Songbook

Songs to Learn & Sing

The Black Book

Fiend Folio

Pretty Monsters

Black Star

I could joke
of thrombosis but this

     frostbite's
for real   like the harm

in the charm if our lips
get eclipsed

    by the flair
    & then the fizzle

    which they're blaming
    on the drizzle

      & how it
    scatters

light, scrambles satellites so they
shush every

     whisper
   lest our fireworks

      ignite
      because life

      isn't bliss,
      life

      is just this
      pause,

      this
      ruse, this plastic

      bag blown by the gusts & so
      we stumble
         & we hush
      but even the slush can seem

      iceberg horizons when our stars
        start to fall

     regardless.

More Songs about Buildings & Food

Crooked man, crooked house. Comes tough & stretch-mouthed, eyes closed & crashing. He wakes slower on the uptake, starts craving simpler sweets. So they break fast &

she draws a square in the air, sings a snatch of "Shortnin' Bread." *Rhombus,* he replies, *molasses fills this hollow earth.* Then they tunnel & door, things unbutton or become

embalmed. In the bedroom, a fray of ravens knocks at walls while outside kites hang tangled from power lines. *Free the silkworms,* he says from his place on the ledge. *Shake*

this hourglass filled with moths. But when she sings a song about a milkshake, his brain goes cotton soft & magnets get somehow swallowed as their robes yawn & the atoms

smash & he stutters & starts to shrink into sleeping, wakes, sleeps more deeply & he's dreaming graven imagery & gravity wells in Escher prints, dragonflies & bubble-briars

& maybe butter drizzled on biscuits. *Grab ass,* he suggests at dawn, *then maybe an almond biscotti. Rope burn,* she replies. *Freezer burn. A touch of reflux, maybe some blind man's bluff.*

The Diamond Sutra

Serpentine sleekness was always my weakness, like a simple tune…

—*Roxy Music, "Mother of Pearl"*

Longfellow Serenade

        O Prolix,
you're horseshoe

to my hand
grenade, hyperbole

despite my over-
writes.

Yesterday's Songs

Homer sings the gods
of war,

Homer sings
"Uptown

Girl." He strings his lyre
w/ piano

wire
if he's got

the notion, molds calliopes
from white

bread then throws them
to the wine-soaked

ocean.

Girl, You'll Be a Woman Soon

She
said, *Rose White,*

*Rose
Red* — & she said,

*Let's pretend
that we're dead —*

& in his head
he's missing Bikini

Kill, he's missing
Urge Over-

kill, he's missing
every avatar

   whose
flash could pan

some sizzle, who
dripped a bit of

   moontan,
lit a candle in his

window.

Song Sung Blue

I.

From his window,
he can see

the little
ballerinas. He asks his

dad, *What does 'in a
minute'*

mean? That last trick,
the old man

whispers, *was simple
misdirection. The next*

*is false
bottoms, then some*

*classic bait &
switch.*

II.

At the Conspiracy
Showroom,

a sweater gets re-
stitched as an

Earth 2 barista
daydreams

of a replicant
who envisions

his own
clone who sits sketching

a black
sheep who works at that

other
Starbucks, the one

right across the
street.

III.

The car alarm was not
the ice cream

man was not the missing
ATM pin & when

the key broke off
in the lock, I opened

                    your diary
using a rock & read all those

notes about Oz
as abstraction but I meant it

in jest, it was just
a distraction.

Solitary Man

I am tripping on my assonance,
I say, *even itching in my iambs.*

Somebody admire my stupid shirt, I say.

I say, *hum in my sternum*
& numb in my arm & portable

stairways, I say,
& low tides & so-

called life rafts, bones filed
to fit the glass slipper.

Play Me

I.

Claymation. Animotion. Obsessive
propulsive: A magic cloud

raining magic flowers. Costumes
in a box. The order already in process,

the slow leak getting quicker.

II.

Clay Aiken. Stop motion. His hand slowed
for no emoticon. Spark Notes

over Cliff Notes, the Time-out Chair
under the Tree of Despair.

III.

Balloon plays music. Balloon
does not fly. Car locked, engine running:

Carve a pumpkin's
tongue

from iron lung.

IV.

Fast Mermaid Lady has pipes like a Chrysler.
Hope

is like licorice. Patience is like La Brea tar.

V.

Common knowledge
as the lowest of limbos. Wall of cardboard bricks

as approximate graffiti. Screaming Green Gorilla
did the Dance Dance Revolution,

left an Etch-
A-Sketch in my teddy bear's

intestines.

VI.

Evolution. Reproduction. Voice box
swiped by a wily

fox, face frozen while miming sneeze
or seizure.

Two-Bit Manchild

Never a feather this sack of bones
like this papier-mâché

in place of my face or that fan
dancer trapped by Mylar

balloons or these people's
demands on my prosthetic

hand or the blowback
of Afrin, the wrong-

frosted cupcakes
& some old man mumbling

something about a dark
Scottish lake.

Stones

I.

Neither touching from
a distance nor kissing

to be clever: rather
this Monroe in

the mirror,
her mouth

sprouting
flowers.

II.

Signify the owl
eyes. Wax

meta-
physical atop

piles of
imported

shirts. Our spots
in time will keep

getting eaten. Our
briar patch

remains thick w/
ticks.

III.

There will be too much grit in our
realism, not enough lasers. There will be

apples laden w/ razor blades,
strychnine in the

lemonade & sleights
       of hand & plastic

             bouquets & when forced
             to choose between two

bales of hay, he'll light a match
& walk away.

The Great American Songbook

I.

Who could forget the schoolyard debates that raged around Phil Collins's "In the Air Tonight"? According to legend, Collins had written the track as but one step in a master plan to avenge the death of a childhood friend, and while my classmates and I were scouring the song's lyrics for traces of Collins's murderous scheme, we were oblivious to a much darker, more sinister pop masterpiece being played in supermarkets and singles' clubs across America, namely Rupert Holmes's "Escape," which is more commonly known by what is actually its parenthetical subtitle, "The Pina Colada Song." If anything, Holmes's 1979 classic delighted young and old alike with its humorous yet tightly structured narrative of two erstwhile adulterers who ultimately realize the perfection of their match based on a chance encounter worthy of a Paul Auster novel: the narrator responds to his own lover's personal ad that she had placed in a local newspaper without his knowledge, an act that ultimately, and against all odds, reaffirms their bond.

In retrospect, however, one might read Holmes's narrative as a disturbed re-envisioning of "Gift of the Magi," a dark, troubling portrait of the free-wheeling '70s swinger culture gone wrong. For instance, one notes that even as the narrator and his nameless "lady" return to the cozy confines of monogamy, they do so based not on a more nuanced understanding of one another's emotional, physical, and spiritual needs but on a shared fondness for alcohol and a disdain for both yoga and health food. Is Holmes perhaps hinting, in a rather diabolical way, that the escape alluded to in the song's full title will come later, as the couple drowns their sublimated dissatisfaction with one another in endless carafes of cheap champagne followed by melancholy strolls in what can only be described as highly symbolic thunderstorms? Indeed, while "Escape" features none of the brooding, echo-laden histrionics of Collins's song, embedded beneath its cheery exterior is a truly perverse narrative made all the more horrible by its ironically catchy melody, just as the sickly-sweet mixed drink for which it is named can still leave one filled with shame and remorse in the cold, inevitable light of dawn.

II.

Mojo Nixon is perhaps best known for his mention in "Punk Rock Girl," a tongue-in-cheek anthem of disaffected youth performed by The Dead Milkmen. However, Nixon has had a 20-year career as a cult musician that peaked sometime in the 80s, when he penned notorious pop culture parodies such as "Debbie Gibson Is Pregnant with My Two-Headed Love Child" and "Stuffin' Martha's Muffin," an off-color ode to then-MTV VJ Martha Quinn. His most scathing track is surely "Don Henley Must Die," which finds fault with the Eagles singer and part-time environmentalist for infractions ranging from angst-laden lyrics to an ill-advised ponytail hairstyle.

One evening, Nixon was performing that very song in an Austin, Texas nightclub when Henley himself strode on to the tiny stage, grabbed a spare microphone, and belted out the tune alongside a flabbergasted Nixon. From that day forth, a chastened Nixon swore he would change the lyrics of the song to "Rick Astley Must Die." Who Astley is (or was) is not the issue; it is simply worth noting that the ease with which Nixon chose to change the lyrics indicates that the sentiment could not have possibly been sincere in the first place. That said, recalling this incident years after the fact, I feel warmly toward both Henley and Nixon for reasons that are somewhat unclear to me, especially since I am not particularly interested in the music of either man.

III.

For many of his fans and even his more casual listeners, the fact that Rod Stewart has been romantically linked to a series of progressively younger women, including his current fiancé, model Penny Lancaster, who is more than 25 years his junior, clearly invalidates the sordid tales of homosexual tomfoolery that dogged Stewart earlier in his career. Any memories of rumors involving trips to the hospital for emergency stomach pumping after a supposed same-sex romp, for instance, are likely invalidated by his wooing and impregnating of supermodel Rachel Hunter in the early 1990s.

The issue of Stewart's sexual orientation is not of interest to me *per se*. However, it is worth pondering how the same man who gave us such hormonal classics as "Hot Legs" and "Do Ya Think I'm Sexy?" is currently offering up banal versions of selections from the Great American Songbook. Granted, these men share the same name, the same raspy, whiskey-soaked voice, and even the same carefully disheveled locks, but little else seems to connect the two entities. The best explanation I can offer is that, as part of the human body's constant process of regeneration, our cells are, in essence, completely replaced every seven years. Therefore, the man butchering "Time After Time" on Oprah Winfrey's couch and the man who once caroused alongside soon-to-be Rolling Stone Ron Wood are, quite literally, not the same person at all.

IV.

I remember once hearing a radio DJ complain that Bryan Adams could not have been old enough to be in a band in 1969, despite claims to the contrary in his first-person narrative "Summer of '69," as if a fictional tale could not possibly contain true emotion or sincerity. The fact that we have such high expectations of the popular music we consume reminds me, somehow, of a moment in U2's self-indulgent documentary *Rattle And Hum*. As the band launches into a credible if unremarkable version of "Helter Skelter," Bono announces to the audience, "Charles Manson stole this song from the Beatles, and we're stealing it back!" "Helter Skelter" has long been a live staple of a wide range of bands, ranging from Mötley Crüe to Siouxsie & the Banshees, so it is curious that Bono — or anyone else, for that matter — could "steal" the song in the first place.

While we may never truly "own" another person's song or even completely understand its complexities, it doesn't stop us from trying. Indeed, Canadian songstress Alanis Morrissete still refuses to reveal the identity of the older lover who inspired her vitriolic, decade-old anthem "You Oughta Know," but at a recent charity event Carly Simon actually auctioned off the name of the man who was the subject of her 1972 hit "You're So Vain," a fact that Simon has always guarded in a coy fashion not unlike Morrissete's current stance. The auction's winner was provided with the name in question on the condition that he, the high bidder, never tell another living soul what he had learned. Imagine, for a moment, the intoxication of having such wealth that you can essentially bribe the writer to take you into her confidence and whisper her secrets in your ear, naïvely trusting that what she's telling you is, in the end, something that approximates the truth.

Songs to Learn & Sing

He was wandering amid obscene
hexameters. He was wondering
about blame & maybe some miniature

golf. His t-shirt advertised ironic
detachment, tried to satirize
prior fits of possession

or maybe rabies. First the bulb
had dropped from its socket & now
his coffee was getting mocked.

His t-shirt said, *Not Dead Yet* & so
Switzerland became metaphor for sabotage
or subterfuge & other stuff that gets swept

under rug. He tried using the word *squash*
as a noun, watched the cloud cover moving
& was, therefore, moved. Perhaps the colony

had not actually collapsed in all that
disorder, he reasoned. Meanwhile his fingers
itched to chop at logic like a tiny white pill.

The Black Book

> ...need need need
> until he went to pieces.
> The pieces sat up & wrote.
>
> —*John Berryman, "Dream Song 311"*

The Black Book is a text of mixed
messages: one minute he's all

New Romantic Bang
Tango, then he turns around

& asks for a bit of the Jacobean
cut &

thrust. Witness him trapped between faux-
spontaneous bead throwing

& full frontal new
deity. Witless him brimming

w/ longings, double-
crosses, aborted stories

   of sorry & sea sick
   & even embittered

   but still the stick
   pin comes

   unstuck.

The Black
Book knows

how it goes: if various,
then sundered,

if delicious, then demolition.
The year punk broke

in half, he shivered
        meat embers

              & sliced at smoke
        of boa

        constrictors,
        let her root-

glimmer slither sidelong
'til sparks arced across

his iris & burned him from
the inside

out.

The Black Book hates the hesitancy of pencils, the numbness of latex.

Written in The Black Book: *Mistakes were made.*

Written in The Black Book: *How thick my blood became.*

But Dyslexic Black Book can't even spell the word *climax*, let alone have one.

When he comes unhinged like this, he's nothing but scratched-out names & out-of-date addresses.

Sometimes he gets so anxious he skips straight to the falling action.

Some nights, he just sits there & Googles you.

The moon
looms. The Black Book slogs

along the sidewalk. He's stooped,
scurvied,

        adrift in sudden squalls &
        fits of cabin fever. Still he

stops to scrawl the occasional page
& slip it through mail slots of

the sleeping, his meditations
on an emergent

sea.

She sells snake broth
& The Black Book bought

it all & shot the wadded
dollars just to watch them

        fall & he thought
        about the piety

& he thought about the fiery
rain & he thought about

the apple pie that's
baking in his

brain.

The Black Book lacks any hint of accident.

In the lexicon of The Black Book, there is no difference between *lack* & *like*.

The Black Book contains the following phrases: *egregious eros, supreme friction, spf XXX*.

Within him are dreams about pears & the politics betwixt & beneath the wax & the tweeze, the cliché of quiche when it's gifted in grief.

The Black Book never
forgets a

      face, embraces
even the Greatest American

Martyr, the Dollar Pollyanna.
He sees their teeth meet

& goes swollen w/ *noblesse oblige*,
declares their groping to be godless

& pure. He already has cake on his
hands &

he wants to trade your fries
for slaw,

      maybe two
      thighs for a

      wing.

Hates the medication
but takes it all the

same. Changed his name
to *Unchained Caveman*,

then changed it back
again. While wasps spin

circles inches from his
skin, some half-chewed

candy corn dribbles
down his

chin.

The Black Book feels your pain. He misses your body, just wants to be held, fears you'll shelve him under "Self Help" & move on.

He wants you to flip his pages & clip passages at random, maybe cut & paste these recycled ciphers until he's finally free from narrative, nothing left but bits of flesh pressed into fresh positions.

Fiend Folio

Are there many little boys who think they are a Monster? But in my case I am right said Geryon to the Dog...

— *Anne Carson,* Autobiography of Red

Albatross

Books
in my jaws,
I talk.

I rail
at my nightingale

in plain
song

sung wrong. My frown

aches adder
from eel, bends sinister
all sparks at will.

The night falls,
the falcon

alights,
tosses the tangled entrails

at the base of my bed.

Botched Chupacabra

I.

Corners
& quick the boards

over the doors.
A thin bit of cotton

shoved aside & hope
croaks over gums

in torn verbs, turpentine.
The same old starch

sewn over every orifice,
the tight smile

pulled tighter
by hidden strings. Taut,

tauter this tinkering
until fit to tear.

II.

Dripping water dropped
to rumor

& sticky hearts
stuck to

wall.
You stew

in stagnant air
& when the hordes move

to drain your humours,
their antlers gore

as a sort of surge
& recur. &

recur. &
recur.

Disinvited

The romance of
shipwreck &

inevitable an eighth day's
fever, some

Stratego mixed
w/ bits of necromancy

& so this mess
you've left,

i.e., attachment
to one's captor, e.g.,

one pissed-off Tinkerbell,
or, c.f.,

another day of nickels,
the countless fallen

robins, et
cetera. *Cannonball*,

the boy calls, & then he leaps
overboard.

Ethan Frome Goes

There was momentum to those
brushstrokes, my landscapes

painted in haste. I tried
to rise. I rose &

grew confused & I was among the lilacs
& the fireflies. Now I'm scratching

at that canvas, pigment scraped
to escape this scene.

Half-Imagined Juju

I.

Rooster
has language.

Rooster has migraine,
hates peacock near henhouse.

Peacock can't speak, peacock
still taps that ass.

II.

The definition of *is* depends
upon

this head full of egg-
shells,

her approximate
wingspan, his soft spot

for crush of hollow
bones.

Kultured Lycans

I.

A Gollum called "Mr. Moonlight,"
shit pellets smearing his floor
in slurry Ouroboros.

II.

The Cyborg says,
Your gods are long gone.

Then she drops her clothes.

"Cyborg" isn't exactly correct,
she says, *but at least you're getting*

close.

III.

These weeds beyond the razor wire, he keens,
*hide castles built by magpies, entire armies
of vermin that shall rise at my command.*

IV.

Continuity demands that the silver bullet stays chambered.

That zippers stay zipped, minor characters disappear unremembered.

That the raptor scrambles backward, arcs unwritten in the afterburn.

Martyrs Need Onanism

Poison sumac out back
means secretions

weeping sweetly
as we snuggle

in the dusk.

Paris

Night blooming narcissus
oblivious to the spit

in its eye. Wakes stiff
& stumbles,

spills sideways
all preening &

puddled,
comes unbloomed in easy

bruises behind the Vicodin
& piled-on bronzer.

You creep closer, pluck its sockets
to see what's inside,

but the blank just
stares back at you, gaping,

shameless,
framed in Gucci.

Quiet

Librarians smell
like marinara. They shush us

wherever we
huddle,

cut out our tongues & wear them
as necklaces,

sew shut our lips w/fishing line,
then they sit there

laughing at us, eating scones,
shopping online.

Rue

I.

A twilight singer, a hyper
ballad. A feeling

of gaze.
So slips the sliver's

envy, a slip of girl
& her broken

branch, a last grasp
at slippery limbs.

II.

Take me
for a sponge,

a flange,
a scaffold for your foil.

She says *admixture*
when *mixture* would do,

supercilious
in place of *jackass*. I say no such

& nonesuch & even this splinter
is of suspicious vintage.

III.

A penny for your thinking,
your thoughts

on bridal eyelids. The maiden
hums her penny dreadfuls, murmurs

from her murk.

IV.

What falls
when we fail these sighs,

these
heaves: the sidewalk up & hit me,

sniffed & spit me out. A neverwhere
for your nohow,

a drowsing
while you drown.

Screaming Trees

I.

We suppose
the roses & suppose the stone,

the stammer,
the stare, the *I swear I bleed*

these dead words in need of tether.
I cut construction paper stars

then sketch an ape,
clearly limping,

his mouthful of feathers
all dusted in blood.

II.

Venture forth from the porch
& risk deflower &

a fever of teeth all about
the neck. I am all ink

until my elbows itch. You favor
porcelain kitties & QuickTime

hipsters. You're a long time gone.
You were never really there.

Ultraviolence

Tiny Vikings break Jane Austen.

They play grab-
ass in class, crash their dad's Stratus

on the weekends. They
come together

in clusters to imagine our overthrow,
gossip about our bad

breath. They creep into our beds
as we sleep, gut us

w/ hunting knives, curl up to nap
wrapped in bloodied sheets.

We Were X

I.

This nervous never-
end,

another version
of supposed somewhats

that somehow suddenly
get all nervous again.

II.

Sheathed means softest,
as in *like* or *as*, as in getting

caught
between the prick songs,

lost beyond the para-
spheres.

III.

Write
the check. Wipe

the eyes. Squeeze,
release, step right

outside.

Yoda

I.

Sand blast the abstractions
full of holes & you know

the devil will wait in those
tiny spaces.

II.

Craft a catchphrase to describe
so deep a cavern. Try

decrepifying, then scratch it out
& try again.

III.

Dear Y.,

As requested, have chronicled the appeal of demons, have categorized following the required guidelines: Fiends of Blasphemy, Fiends of Corruption, Fiends of Possession. Have many questions. Pls advise.

IV.

A waxworks of disembodied
heads. A lullaby

to paralyze, to re-cork Pandora
& un-

carve Pygmalion's parlor game.

V.

I wrote *disembodied* but meant *severed*.

Apologies for any confusion.

VI.

Dear Y.,

Code Name Erato is now in play. Pls send backup. Request Ganesh, but will accept Gilgamesh, Green Arrow, a lesser Power Ranger if necessary.

Zenith

Snake in aviary caught starling
off guard while swallow

squashed lizard out in our
backyard as canary

shattered skylight
when tomcat

napped & now
she's going

supernova,
exploding

into sun.

Pretty Monsters

I.

The Sherpa says, *Pulse & push out the inside.*

He says, *The second truffle comes at the end.* Then he pauses to shuffle the playlist.

He says, *Your brain is wired for spikes, but the patterns can be reconceived. You have to bend & lift until you burn, then keep bending & lift again.*

He says, *When sharks die, they sink head first, sort of on a diagonal, until they end up with their skulls stuck in the sand.*

He says, *I know this sounds suspicious.* Then he disappears.

        We run from room to room, never seeing how the walls reconfigure behind us. Hallways are elongating, stairs disappearing beneath our feet, & we have come back to the starting point, smears of phosphorous marking our recent descent.

II.

Each season is a new mission,
is full of flare gun &

tourniquet & entire cities
smashed by sudden

squalls. We have drained the lake
to keep you from drowning,

siphoned gas to prevent
explosion. Still there are questions

about blood infections, about radiation
& half life

& how night lights keep demons safely
outside.

III.

The Hydra asks, *Is anybody hurt?*

She asks, *Does he want his mother?*

She snaps, *Which one of you broke this mirror, anyway?*

She sighs, *Well, you never know these days.* Then she walks away.

IV.

We prefer pullies
& ladders,

bridges that suspend
gravity. We like to jump puddles

in new boots. We like pieces of things
from which to weave

a dreaming.

V.

The Firewall says, *Open your eyes. Don't take a breath. Open your eyes. Hand me that suitcase. Don't breathe. Hand me that DVD. I said don't smile. I said don't take a breath.*

VI.

Scared of shadows & scarred by
turtles & always this

spider
at the edge of the text.

You scream the air
inward, become rubber

even as I squeeze. You recover
from upside

down & demand a bigger
engine.

VII.

The Conductor asks, *What do satyrs eat?*

The Conductor says, *The cougar is loose in the backseat, the specter ready to enter the machine.*

VIII.

Tents built amid
the wreckage &

an outpost between two
riverbeds,

these blessings written
not in sand

but atop vanilla cake.

IX.

The Chocolate Chicken says, *You're my best friend. Now smell my hand.*

The Chocolate Chicken says, *Call me "Mr. Riddles."*

I say, *OK.*

Mr. Riddles says, *I like to crackle through the wires. I leave the climbing to others.*

X.

Before the lights go out, you ask for Typhon
& Echidna & then your favorite happy

endings & so we let these myths
blend, wending paths of bread

crumbs never eaten,
enchantments

never cast &
this way, then, our odyssey

never ends, our oracle
never poisoned

after
all.

Chris McCreary is the author of two previous full-length collections, *The Effacements* (Singing Horse Press) and *Dismembers* (ixnay press), in addition to several chapbooks, including *Sansom Agonistease* (Potes & Poets Press). Along with his wife Jenn McCreary, he has co-edited ixnay press for over a decade, publishing numerous chapbooks, eight issues of *ixnay* magazine, and four installments of a "mini-anthology" entitled *the ixnay reader*. (Much of the press's output is now available as free pdf files at ixnaypress.com.)

Chris has reviewed fiction, poetry, and poetics for venues such as *Rain Taxi*, *The Poetry Project Newsletter*, *The Philadelphia Inquirer*, and *Review of Contemporary Fiction*, and he has published his own short fiction in *New Review of Literature* and elsewhere. He holds an MA in Creative Writing from Temple University, and he teaches at a private high school outside of Philadelphia, where he lives with Jenn and their twin sons.